Endless Journey

Endless Journey

Sumedha Jena

BLACK EAGLE BOOKS
2020

BLACK EAGLE BOOKS

USA address:
7464 Wisdom Lane
Dublin, OH 43016

India address:
E/312, Trident Galaxy, Kalinga Nagar,
Bhubaneswar-751003, Odisha, India

E-mail: info@blackeaglebooks.org
Website: www.blackeaglebooks.org

First International Edition Published by
BLACK EAGLE BOOKS, 2020

ENDLESS JOURNEY
by **Sumedha Jena**

Copyright © **Sumedha Jena**

All rights reserved. No part of this publication may be reproduced, stored in a retrieval system, or transmitted, in any form or by any means, electronic, mechanical, photocopying, recording or otherwise without the prior permission of the publisher.

Cover Art: **Sandhya Jena**
Interior Design: Ezy's Publication

ISBN- 978-1-64560-073-2 (Paperback)
Library of Congress Control Number: 2020936997

Printed in United States of America

Dedicated To

My Maternal Grandfather
Late Durga Prasad Jagatdeo
and
My Paternal Grandmother
Late Suprava Jena

Editor's Note

I have the pleasure of going through twenty one poems by a young poet, Sumedha Jena, written mostly in quartlets. The nostalgic longing for discovering the self is unmistakable in these poems. A dream like quality runs through almost all these poems. The first person narrative makes the poems poignant. However, there are a few poems written in third person narrative. The poet very rightly says, "Our dreams are our realities lay awaiting" ('Dream'.) The poetic persona in quite a few poems plays the victim card waiting to be redeemed . The longing comes to an end when she says, "But then I met you" ('a dark moon'.) Even then, the fear continues to haunt the protagonist.

She says,
>"I am scared.
>Three words I repeat daily...
>My fear is getting the best of me."
>
>('too scared')

One of the last few poems, "Cave " is a thought provoking poem. Searching for answers to one's questions in life is a perennial problem. Answers may come and also may not. The search continues and that is the enigma of human life.

The language of the poems is compact as well as the thought content. This young poet is full of promise and potential. She has the poetic voice which one day would take her to a new height.

Dr. Bijay Kumar Das, Ph.D, D Litt.
Professor of English (Retd.)
The University of Burdwan
Burdwan, West Bengal, India

Preface

I started writing poetry when I was about nine years old, and it was my grandparents who saw some potential in me. I was writing small poems for fun, or whenever I felt a strong sense of emotion. Once I started showing them to my family, they thought it would be good to see a writer in our family. My grandfather is a writer, and my family wanted me to grow to become like him. They always tried to push me to write as much as I could at the age. As I grew a little older, I realized that I didn't want to be a writer and have that as my career. However, even if I didn't want to become a writer, I could always have it as a hobby. There was even a period of time, when I had gone through writer's block and I wasn't able to think of anything creative at all. Nevertheless, my parents continued to encourage me to write so I would be able to publish a book one day. I was able to finish what I had started earlier. By having my family besides me, I was able to publish my first book ever.

A majority of the poems written in this book aren't from my own experiences, rather they are from seeing other people experience something similar. A lot of the poems are also exaggerated to give the reader a better understanding and insight about what they're reading. At a young age, I realized that life is not always a happy journey, and that one has to always endure hardships along the way in order to reach a successful point in their life.

I wrote these poems targeting anybody who has gone through something similar in life. I felt like if I write poetry based on these topics, someone might be able to relate to them. This book is basically about the transition of coming out of a dark, angry, and an unhappy place into a more radiant world. At first, I was writing these poems whenever I felt extreme anger of sadness. But, as I kept writing I saw that many of my poems had a similar theme, and it was all negative. I didn't want to write poetry that was just filled with sadness. So, I started writing poems that showed the change from sad to happy. Most people don't even understand the burden of going through all of this. I tried to bring these topics to light, by turning them into poetry. I apologize, if any of the poems trigger anybody. I did not write this to anger anybody, but only to shine a light on the issues that kids, teenagers, and even adults face. I hope my readers will go through the poems and provide me criticism and feedback to refine my thought process.

I would like to first thank my parents and my grandparents for always supporting me and motivating me to write. They were there for me, when nobody else was. I also want to thank my editor Dr. Bijay Kumar Das, who helped perfect this book. He had taken valuable time out of his busy schedule to review the poems and give me very important suggestions.

CONTENTS

Isolation	17
Go Away	20
Too Scared	22
Cave	24
An Imaginary Friend	26
Alert	28
Heavy Hearts	29
Submerge	30
Repair Me	31
Escape	33
There's no one	35
Dream	37
Rain	39
Once Upon A Time	41
A Cycle Of Change	43
A Winter Solstice	45
One Summer Ago	46
A Dark Moon	49
The Little Things	51
Sunflower Child	53
Happy	55

She blamed herself constantly
The puzzles didn't fit together
Every night and day
All she could hear was yelling

Neither of them wanted her
No longer part of anything or anyone
Doesn't know what makes her happy anymore
She is sinking into her own mind
She needs someone to save her
From her destructive mind

Every thought of hers is a battle
Every battle is a war
And she knows for a fact
That she will always lose

Neglected from her family and friends
No one comes to her to hold her hand
And take her someplace
Somewhere other than here

She gets lost in her mind
Becomes invisible to others
She's drowning in her thoughts
The immerse waves take her in

She knows she isn't gone yet
But she blames herself for everything
If she can find the light
She can still smile

She built her walls very high
She didn't want to let anybody in
They would learn every dark secret about her
She didn't want anyone to know

It's definitely not the end
She keeps moving forward
One step at a time
She still has a long way to go
I am cracked. Not broken

Go Away

Another day gone
Left without looking back
You did what you did
There is no fixing that

No reason no cause
A rift with another
Constantly ask myself
Why another mistake

I thought I knew you
But I was wrong
Every word you said was a lie

You started and I followed
Words spread like wildfire
it pained me like a thousand knives
Stabbing me in the back

It was a lot to take in
When I realized
I only existed to you
When you needed something

You took what you needed
I got tossed to the side
And just stayed there and decayed

After everything you have done
I felt overused
I just wanted to walk out

When I looked at you
I feel the urge to say a word
To get back our friendship
Then it hits me
You weren't who you said you were

I don't want you walking back
Pretending everything's okay

If you do ever come back
No more fake apologies
Instead of being there
You decided to leave without a reason

Thinking you were different
Than everyone else
It's okay that you left
Just don't ever come back

Too Scared

I am scared.
Three words I repeat daily
So many things to be afraid of
There is one thing
That rips my nerves from my body
I fear the monster hiding underneath
Demons howling during the dead night
Falling off the edge of the world
Isn't that haunting
Fearful of losing my loved ones
Anxious of the world dying
It never comes to an end
Scared of suffocating by the strong tides
Another one is getting lost in the sea
There is darkness enclosing me
No exit in my mind
My fear is getting the best of me
There's no place to hide
I am locked in my thoughts
Another fear captured
I let it consume me
And now it's cold, gloomy, and deep
My fear looks like the dark corner of a street
And sounds like wind howling at night
I push people away when I get scared

I am scared of being rejected
When I am not accepted
I am afraid of being alone with the trees
I fear the wild creatures hiding out there
My fear has succumbed me
to someone I am not
And now I am a different person
Someone who is only made up of fear

Cave

Boats stirring above the black sea
Grappling hooks slashing into the water
It shudders when he hears them
being pulled up
It doesn't want to be one of them

It hides itself into the cave
For it doesn't want to be seeked by them
They are all now taken away
So all it does is sit in silence

He looks at all of his friends
The ones that were sheared
In the bottom of a shallow sea
Encrusted with the iridescent shells

That's all the view it has
It can't go above the water and look
And look at the view
For all it is stuck beneath

It scratches the walls of the empty cave
Piercing the ears of anyone near
The honed teeth of the creature
No one can stare at it for too long

Poison seeps out from the cracks of the cave
Waiting to catch its next prey
The creature just sits inside the emptiness

It calls the fish its friends
Sometimes they would just come to him
But he knew the real reason why
They were scared of him and he is too

He is long lost in the midnight zone
With no light able to pass by
He knows he is safe inside his cave
Let alone that everyone is dead

But sometimes he just wishes
That he could just swim out there
Wanting to show everyone
That he won't hurt them

Is it the creature
Is it him that's affected
Or is it me
I ask but no one answers

An Imaginary Friend

Getting lost in thoughts that were never there
But she was always hiding somewhere
Playing around with my mind
Hiding secrets that I could never find

She always got me in trouble
For things I never did
Was always with me
Through my journey as a kid

Unaware of what I saw but I think it was her
Following me everywhere like a shadow
Appearing in my dreams and my nightmares
Prancing away in the sunflower meadow

They always told me that she wasn't real
That I didn't have any friends
Besides my imaginary one
Since she did whatever I told her

They made fun of me since I was young
No one really understood me
I was caged. I wasn't free
But there she was staring at me

The moment I realized
She wanted to be my friend
I knew that this wasn't the end
All I could say was that I had someone

Nobody else saw her except me
Everyone saw right through her
We would play and play
At night and all day

That time came when I grew old
She became distant and isolated
Never spoke another word
She's an imagination they all told me

Deep inside I knew she wasn't real
But she would always stay with me
Always there whenever I needed her
Slowly becoming my other half

One day she disappeared
There was no response from her
She left without a trace
Never came back for a glance

Ridiculed and teased
I stopped caring too much
My friend still didn't come
She's an imagination they said

Alert

Dispiriting nights
I will lie awake alone
To the monster near

Isolation

The feeling of blood racing
Hammering in her chest
It was roaring back
They were speechless and empty

Sadness came over her like a black cloud
There was a gaping hole in her chest
She thought that she'd be in a closed box
But she knew she could outlast a million men

She had no light of her memory
She had no road to change
Everything was a coalish black
And all she saw was the yellow moon

She kept her thoughts to herself
As no one understands them anyway
She doesn't get why she is confused
As to why people left her

She noticed everything around her
And just acted like she didn't
She couldn't sleep for several nights
Because her mind kept racing

Heavy Hearts

The glorious nature of sympathy
Sending my condolences for your tragedy
Understanding what you been through
As I can say I have been through the same
I share your feelings
And I hope you return the same
I am there to remove the dead feelings
In hopes to give you the love you deserve
I live only to remove your eternal sufferings
Of the unfair cruel world
Please don't shed tears
They will live in your pure heart
It will bend and break
But it will never forget
Don't be a caged bird
Waiting to be set free into the cyan world
Soaring into the blustery winds
I bid you goodbye

Submerge

How does it feel when we jump
Into a depthless pool
Filled with overweight feelings
Pulling me into a perplexing center

Gravitating me when I fall underwater
Unable to breathe
My throat suddenly dense
Choking on invisible air

Dreaming in my cerulean dress
Or is it a surreal reality
Oblivious to what's near me
So I slowly sink below

Blurred visions are in my present mind
My sanity is therefore illusive
Blank state of an unconscious mind
Filling up with black water

How does it feel to jump
I ask you this daily
As I cough up a silent scream
And submerge with your intrusive dreams

Repair Me

I was sewn together, thread by thread
until a finger decides to pull me apart.
Separated from what I was made up of
I find myself plummeting to the floor.

Days passed, as did weeks
Nobody came to put me back together
I became weary and old
Figured I was to no use

Looked up and I saw
A shadow hovering over me.
She picked me up and starts to sew
Becoming something entirely different

Happy and assured
Hoping to stay like this forever

Two hands swiftly pick me up
and started to tug and pull.
My hope was shattered
Disappeared for good

Pulled and pulled until I started to tear

Next thing I know
I find myself in two pieces and thrown away
Had nothing to lose, so I simply waited
Waited for a kind soul to repair me once again

Escape

She's trapped in a world
And she can't escape her mind
Imaginations unfurled
Feelings unable to be controlled

It feels like a labyrinth
Overcrowded with webbed lies
Her thoughts make her scream and shout
Nobody can hear her beyond her cries

Wanting to escape to a place
Left without a single trace
Wishing to escape from reality
Cause she dreams of a paradise

She is engulfed by the darkness
Deep breaths and salty tears
Words eating her from inside
Lost within the chaos on the street

Every night she thinks about
The thoughts that swallow her whole
Wandering. Never knowing where to go
She is left to make the decision
Not knowing how to choose

Battling her mind every day.
She is slowly spiraling downwards
Her demons may act silent
But they never leave her alone

Always looking for an excuse
To whisper in her ear
Needing enough strength
To make herself sane again

Left in a confused state
Full of maniac episodes
She did not want to see their judgment
Did not want to change herself anymore

Stronger than she was ever
She couldn't let herself crumble anymore

There's no one

Walking down the broken path
Trees shadowing the distant road
I am abandoned and afraid
Nobody can find me

I am stuck in a maze
With all exits blocked
The voices whisper my name
Memories are hazy as they fade away

It's been days since I was gone
Nobody has called
No one noticed I was gone
Can't get my voice to speak out

Surrounded by never ending darkness
I have fallen into an abyss
The sun has set for dusk
The moon has risen for night

The stars are my company
Everything speaks quiet
No sound to be heard for miles
I am kept silent

I dream that I will be raised
From this bottomless pit
The rain falls in
tapping 'hello' to my hollow head

My smile is stolen from my face
I am afraid to stand in this place
There is no one to talk to
Constant fear wraps its arms

There are always worse things
Than being alone
But loneliness is the only thing I have
Right here and right now

The pain came to an end
The days are unbelievably irradiant
The stars have slept
There is a summery feeling in the air

It's time to be alive again

Dream

I fall into the fortress of thoughts
No longer conscious of the world surrounded
My visions are blurred between the lines
Within the worlds of reality and fantasy

Reliving a fragment of a memory
Over and over again
Abstract colors fill my head
Painting a picture that was never there

A broken mirage
Quiet whispers drawing me in
Into a spiral of crowded ambitions
With the wings of a bird it slowly flies away

Watching it gleam on the crown on my head
My fragile conscious afraid to break
When the dream doesn't fester
No one's there for it to mend

A stagnant stream however disappointing
As it flows from the ocean of words
Our dreams are our realities lay awaiting
While we plant the seeds to a future unseen

All dreamers paint a picture
They hold onto their perfect aspirations
Before it becomes engulfed
By a blanket of dismay and sorrow

Waiting to fling my arms in the radiating sun
Hoping that it never goes gloomy

While an opportunity in disguise
Stretching towards the expanding horizon
Boundless and limitless as I soar
In the sky with a single intention

A beautiful relapse
Suddenly awakens me
And I lie alone but arouse

Back in the comfort of my pillows
Unaware of the vivid reminiscence
All I'd ever known
Was all just a pensived dream

Rain

Calming winds with a sudden rage
Glowing eyes flashing anger
Silver droplets hitting the sheer window
The thundering noise of the clouds above

A wavered light shines its way through
Blinding whoever sets its eyes upon it
Leaves come dancing down
Hitting the ground while the water streams

A cooling breeze swept across my face
The ground now vulnerable
Lashing out on a lonely stranger
Walking down the cobblestone street

My eyes gaze out the window in summer heat
Into the tornado of leaves
The colors slowly wash out
Into a crumbling gray world

Smoldering blues melting with green
Bellowing its melancholy tune
Bestrewing the blossoms underneath
Destroying anything in its way

Falls to ground with an angel's touch
Giving another life
I watch as the earth submerges
Into a world where you can't breathe

A place once silent
Filled with the words of a bird
Now replenished with a persistent noise
Thrumming on my rooftop

Once afraid of what it might bring
I now walk out as it hits
Melting away in its presence
Letting out a warm smile

As I watch the others dance with me

Once Upon A Time

Walking into one of my favorite places
Holding my cup of coffee
I gaze into an empty space
As the words call out to me

Opening the cover
Im suddenly deluged by its inside

One day i'm alone
Another day i'm with my friends
These colorful characters
Who watched me thrive and grow

Were there for me when I fell
When I became the classic Alice
And fell down my endless rabbit hole
A new chapter in my life suddenly opens

The words seemingly run off
Chasing them to write my own story
I get lost within its vibe
Vibrant but devoid of any color

I keep running onto each page
Looking out in the paper world

The smell of smoulder ignites my thoughts
I run far away before it singes me

Taking a leap I stumble
Into the enchanted forest
I walk until I see the yellow brick road
Every step opening a golden gate

Watching everything come to life
I am now deaf to my surroundings
Left my dull world behind
Looking for a home which no one can find

Something so seemingly unreal
Yet so admiringly eristic
Falling deep into my own fairytale
A hint of fantasy in the air

I get pulled out of my world
Full of make-believe
Dragged into the world of sane
I feel like I am no longer safe

I seeked shelter in those crinkled pages
It was a mystified delight
Back from my own universe
Hidden from a painful reality

The capability of those pages
Were strong enough
To devour me whole

A Cycle Of Change

A frosty blanket wraps the earth with its arms
Terrified. Flora and fauna
Go hide away into the dark
Relentless blizzards show their wrath
Heavy hails come and go
The snow feels isolated from the rest
Time moves leisurely

Blossoms open up their eyes
To a fresh new world
Birds trill their dulcet song
Rays of the buoyant sun
Caress the verdant ground
Empty trees are dressed with flamboyant leaves
Flowers burst with incessant happiness
Spring has put the spirit of youth
Into my juvenile soul

The rousing rain wash my thoughts out
Trees start to dance
With the sultry summer air
Gritty sand comes between my toes
The touch of the ocean tingle my fingers
Joyous moments among my friends

Leaves start to fall
The trees and ground start to wither
The smell of pumpkins fill the air
A cold breeze pushes itself against others

The ground is frozen with fear
Plants start wilting, the grass can't sway
The cycle of change is here for the better
And the blissful life to continue as ever

A Winter Solstice

Bird flies in spring night
Empty bed and sweet goodbyes
Snow cloaks voiceless now

One Summer Ago

One step at a time
Onto the sandy beach
Warmness overwhelming my senses
Flooding with newfound happiness

I write my name in the sand
As the piercing water washes it over
Assorted shells pricking my feet
The smell of boardwalk food impales me

The summer heat with a warm glow
Flaring with a fiery passion
The days become endless and infinite
While the nights became dreamy and magical

I would sit in my backyard
Staring at the cloudless sky
As the scorching sun bathes me
But I run back inside
As I'm drenched like the rain with sweat

Running barefoot across an empty grassy field
With the breezy wind blowing through my hair
Flowers bloomed with beautifully
What a time to be alive

Another time I'd sit by the poolside
Throw my feet in the refreshing water
Scent of the grilled and sizzling burgers
It's heavenly smell took me away

The nights were the best part
When the bright lights wind down
Huddled underneath our sleeping tents
Gazing towards the starry night sky

The blistering heat cools off
As we all jump into the glassy lake
Cheery voices fill the air
An unforgettable moment

The next day the world felt muggy
The ground beneath us was an emerald green
Wishing for an endless summer
We say our final goodbyes
To a youthful time

A Dark Moon

Once was a feeling
Now a part of my soul
A burden on my shoulders
Just never letting go

Feeling like the whole world
Was resting on my shoulders
An overused phrase
But how I felt just never set free

Looking at anyone happier
Ignited a desirous fire
A disease in need of cure
Reminded that I was never enough

Feeling overused and worn
I set off to rest myself to sleep
I wanted to be at ease
But I found it difficult day by day

But then I met you
Pulling me from a dark space
An opaque mind suddenly clear
My belief suddenly agape

I follow you out of the dark
And running into the light
I chase after you in hope
I will be away from night

A sudden rush of euphoria
Immersing my systems
A sense of stability
I was able to walk on my own

A blurry and hazy figure
Not knowing what you were
I knew you were right for me
A lost idea or someone in distress

You questioned the possibility
Of my agonizing existence
And I want to hold your hand
But it falls through

I see right into you
There I am in your mind
Seeing what you saw in me
An image of a scarlet red

Fiery with a raving nature
But inside it glows white
Pure at its glowing heart
And I leave your mind into mine

And I leave happily
Into the world I shine radiantly
Leaving my red and into my white
I thank you for letting you be mine

For turning me into someone
I once aspired to be

The Little Things

Something so small means something so big
Living for those morning sunsets
Life being alluring with every gift it gives
With the little moments in life
Making an entire eternity feel complete

Drops of water makes the boundless ocean
One note produces a beautiful song
Small unnoticed memories
Making up the bigger parts of life

Smallest amount of happiness
Will mean the world to one person
Little acts of kindness
Small words full of love
Rather live in the moment
Then dwell on the past

Live for the morning sunrise
And the alluring evening sunsets
The ones that make you smile
With the ones that brighten up your soul

Living life to the fullest
And enjoy every moment pass
Surrounded by the people you cherish
While you drive with the windows down
And the wind blowing in your hair

Enjoy the warm sun hitting your face
The meadow of flowers on the ground
Breathe in the crisp evening air
Finding joy in the little things

Grains of dirt make up the earth
Small amounts of thoughts making new dreams
One sunbeam lightens up the awakening world
A single tree becomes the start of a vast forest

Deep conversations and long drives
Bringing two and two closer together
It's the little things in life
That make life an adventure

Sunflower Child

Pools of honey in her eyes
Smiling from the aftertaste of his warm smile
Taking in his beauty upon herself
Like a single sunbeam on a summer day

More precious than gold
Smiling immensely brighter than the sun
Her shadow falls over the rest
They all gaze upon it in wonder

Breathing in life and letting go
Days become lingering and mellow
The night brings the frigid and crisp
The piercing pain that would brings

Yellow petals pushing past the green
Pluck you from the ground
Life is drained out painlessly
Blowing the air back in slowly

So vivid and thoughtless
Yet so young and fragile
And one harmful touch will break her
Just admire you from afar

A beautiful blessing
Makes you come back for more
Pulls you into a trance
Hooked onto the numb feeling

Growing roots deep and wide
Has her face staring at the sun
Its delicate heart floats
Dancing through waves of leaves

They are mirrors of glory
Pining for the light of the sun
Is where she strives to be
Unaware of the passing of time

And when it dies
All of the sunshine is gone
Clouds become a bitter gray
Winds start to push and blow

Sometimes it doesn't stay for long
And sometimes it does
Just like a sunflower
It's all temporary

But it still brings me happiness

Happy

The best stories get told
When we go through a long journey
Leaving the black hole behind
That absorbs us completely

Once you walk right in
There is no leaving from there
A rainstorm of sorrow
It was an unnatural feeling

Calmly and gradually I grew
From someone unsteady
To somebody tenacious
Time healed me gently

It was worth waiting for
Surrounded by the people I love
I am truly happy with myself

www.ingramcontent.com/pod-product-compliance
Lightning Source LLC
Chambersburg PA
CBHW021133080526
44587CB00012B/1267